POWER-FILLED PARENTING

THE ETERNITY CONNECTION

Timeless Truths that are Practical for Today and Propelling for Tomorrow

Carol A. Halvorsen, M.A.

Cover Art: Kimberly Sponaugle

Information Processing Model by Sharon R. Berry, Ph.D., used with written permission of the author.

Scripture taken from the HOLY BIBLE, NEW INTERNATIONAL VERSION. Copyright © 1973, 1978, 1984 International Bible Society. Used by permission of Zondervan Bible Publishers.

Library of Congress Control Number: 2004112670

ISBN: 1-883520-27-4

Copyright © 2005 Carol Halvorsen. 2005. All rights reserved. No part of this material may be reproduced, stored in a retrieval system, or transmitted in any form or by any means—electronic, mechanical, photocopying, recording, or otherwise, without written permission of the author.
Printed in the United States of America.

DEDICATION

It is my joy to dedicate this parenting book to my parents. God has blessed me abundantly through them, and I am eternally grateful. Thank you, Mom and Dad, for your love and commitment to the Lord to raise a family on Biblical principles.

A great big thank you goes to Peg, Cathy and Kristy. Thank you for using your editing gifts and skill on this project. Thank you for doing it for the eternal glory of God.

My prayer is that this book will encourage many parents' hearts. It is also my prayer that God will use the truth presented here to transform families into the Godly homes that He desires them to be. God is pleased to pour out His blessing on those who seek Him and keep His commands. Thank you, Lord, for giving us your Word, your Son, and all that we need for life and Godliness in this world and in the world to come.

~Contents~

Introduction: Power-Filled Parenting	5
1 Misconception #1	7
2 Misconception #2	9
3 Misconception #3	13
4 The Biblical View	15
5 The Biblical Couple	18
6 P = Parenting Par-Excellence and Prayer	23
7 A = Authoritative Advocate	26
8 R = Respected Regulator	31
9 E = Eternal Emphasis	46
10 N = Natal Nurturer	50
11 T = Team Teaching	59
12 The Redemptive Heart of God	62
Important Information	66
Resources	74

Introduction

POWER-FILLED PARENTING

Wouldn't it be wonderful if we had Jesus living in our home as our very own personal parenting provost? We can! "How's that?" you may wonder. Well, Jesus says in Revelation 3:20, "If anyone hears *M*y voice and opens the door, I will come in and eat with him, and he with *M*e." If you have invited Him in, He's in! And not only is He living in you, He has given you His Word, *The Bible*, for direction and the Holy Spirit to guide you into all truth (John 16:13). Now that is wonderful!

When we address the issue of parenting and building healthy families, we are really talking about relationships. The first relationship then that must be addressed is the one with Christ Jesus Himself. Romans 10:9-10 states, "That if you confess with your mouth, 'Jesus is Lord,' and believe in your heart that God raised *H*im from the dead, you will be saved. For it is with your heart that you believe and are justified, and it is with your mouth that you confess and are saved." It's that simple; however, it is anything but simplistic. Christ paid the ultimate price by surrendering His life on the cross for us. When we come to the end of ourselves, and we realize that we can't do this thing called life on our own, our eyes are opened and we come to see how much we need a Savior. We are then in a place where God can scoop us up in His loving arms as we acknowledge that Christ died for our sins. We must then surrender our will to His. We can know His will by knowing His Word, the Bible.

This book is designed to help us look at parenting from God's perspective (what He says in the Bible) versus the way the world says that we should raise our children. Keep in mind that the world does not want to be told what to do. It does not want to accept any standards or absolutes. It does not want to live according to God's principles. It believes in freedom to do its own thing, without being accountable to anyone. The Christian also believes in freedom, freedom *from* sin, not freedom *to* sin.

Let's begin with three misconceptions that seem to "rule" family life these days.

Writer's note: Bible verses with **bold** and *italic* marks are added by the author for emphasis, and are therefore not a part of the original NIV text. You will find that all references to God and Godliness are capitalized to give God the honor that is due Him, and to make a clear distinction from any god of this world. Any reference to God's enemy will be lower case, i.e. "satan." Let's be mindful to exalt the Name of The Lord whenever we can.

Chapter One

MISCONCEPTION #1:

RAISING HEALTHY KIDS
vs
"HAPPY" KIDS

The Bible gives clear guidelines for healthy family living. It is the best parenting book ever written. The world, on the other hand, gives false hope for family function. It says: "Buy this" or "Go here" or "Do this." It is all very "thing oriented." For when you do these things, everyone will be happy, and after all, that's what we want. Right?

"Happiness" is a worldly concept or lifestyle. The smallest part of the word is "hap," just like in *hap*penstance or per*hap*s or *hap*penings. Something *hap*pens to me or around me. It is momentary, fleeting. When the happy feelings wear off, you will need something else to keep you "happy," something else, something more, something bigger, or something better. It's a vicious, vicious cycle.

But what people are really looking and longing for is a deep sense of inner well-being. We are looking for that which delights us and enables us to have an optimistic view (positive feeling) on life. We want something that will bring us pleasure, contentment, and peace, even when things aren't so good. The Bible calls this **JOY**! And JOY can only be found in a relationship with the Lord Jesus Christ!

You see, when God created us, He created in us a place where He would live. When He is not filling that place, there is a feeling of emptiness. There's a hunger in the soul that needs to be filled, and it can't be filled with anyone or anything other than the living Christ. When that place isn't filled with Christ, people try to satisfy the longing with things or money, or they resort to dulling the pain in various ways, usually with substance abuse.

Jesus says in John 15:11, "I have told you this so that *M*y joy may be in you and that your joy may be complete." And Paul talks about a "mystery" in Colossians 1:27. He writes, " . . . God has chosen to make known . . . the glorious riches of this mystery, which is *Christ* **IN** you, the hope of glory!" When Christ so floods our being, there is JOY! Real, long-lasting, satisfying JOY!

Our only hope of raising healthy kids and developing healthy families is to be CHRIST-FILLED! Then the longing for momentary pleasures ("happiness") disappears.

Chapter Two

MISCONCEPTION #2:

BUILDING BOUNDARIES
vs
BEING BUDDIES

God has provided many truths and guidelines in Scripture for proper "boundaries." Proverbs is filled with wise sayings that will serve as "protectors" for our children when they are applied.

The commands (rules, regulations) in the Bible are not meant to be "restrictions," although that's what the world will tell you. Instead, they are for our protection.

Proverbs 25:28 states, "Like a city whose walls are broken down is a man who lacks self-control." If a city does not have fortified walls, there is no protection; it is easy prey for the enemy to come in and destroy its inhabitants. Christian, beware! We have an enemy who is prowling around like a roaring lion seeking someone to devour (1 Peter 5:8). We need protection! Since it is the devil who is our enemy, we need God to be our protector. We must call on God in prayer, and we must use His mighty Sword (the Bible) as our greatest weapon. We must spend time in God's Word getting to know our artillery and how to use it. 1 Peter 5:8 begins with, "Be self-controlled and alert." How can we be self-controlled? By reading, knowing, and living according to God's standards.

God's Word tells us that His commands are **not** burdensome (1 John 5:3). "For these commands are a **lamp**, this teaching is a **light**, and the corrections of discipline are the way to **life**" (Proverbs 6:23). Jesus said in John 10:10, "I have come that they may have life, and have it to the full." How does this happen? By knowing the truth, and the *Truth* will set you free! (John 8:32.) There are two things that are described in Scripture as truth: Jesus and His Word (John 14:6, Psalm 119:160). So, as we get to know Christ and the Bible, we can apply truth to our lives, thereby living according to God's standard. As a result we learn to be self-controlled and live in the protection of Almighty God.

There seems to be a paradox here: freedom in boundaries. Jesus said, "Take My yoke upon you . . . " (Matthew 11:29). The yoke of Christ is His moral instruction for us. He says that His way is the easy way. Why? Because He walks beside us and pulls the weight for us. He guides us and He enables us. There is freedom, protection, and provision in "Christ's corral," within His boundaries and fences.

Therefore, we must put into practice the guidelines of Scripture so that we, and our children, can live in accordance with God's will, for that is where we will find protection.

"Being Buddies" with our children is the world's idea. It sounds great, but it removes the authority and respect that God established from the beginning. You are the parent. **Children are to esteem (honor) their parents, not to be equal to them.** Children are not our "buddies," nor can they be our emotional support. When our relationship with our spouse is lacking, or we don't have that close friend to share with, we tend to look to our children to meet our adult emotional needs. Unknowingly, we might start depending on them for our emotional support. They cannot meet those needs. They are not adults; they are children.

We want our children to like us. If they are not happy, we are not happy. We may assume that their unhappiness is our fault. We might believe that we have done something wrong or that we are depriving them of something important. Sometimes we are just too tired to deal with a situation, and we give in to their wishes. We don't like to see our children upset. We don't want to hear the crying or yelling, so we find the quickest, easiest solution to stop the madness. If we are truly honest, it has really become "all about me." We ask: "What's easiest for me?" or "What will help my child like me?" or "What was it that I was lacking growing up that I want to see different for my child?" The list, questions, and reasons are endless.

God's Word gives great guidelines (instructions, commands) for Godly parenting. It is hard work but well worth the time and energy. The payoff will be huge in the life of your child. As your children grow and mature, they will be able to build their homes on a solid foundation, which will then be passed on to the next generation. What's more, is that living according to God's *boundaries* invites His *blessings* into our homes (Deuteronomy 30:15-20).

Chapter Three

MISCONCEPTION #3:

SAVORING FAMILY TIME
vs
SURVIVING FRANTIC SCHEDULES

Chapter 5 of Deuteronomy lists the *Ten Commandments*, which is God's moral law for us. As we continue reading in chapter 6, we find out how to teach these in our homes, the premise being that we actually have time at home as a family. It says in verse 7, "Impress them on your children. Talk about them when you sit at home and when you walk along the road, when you lie down and when you get up." This means that we should diligently teach, point out, and whet their appetites for truth. It means that we should be making time to be with each other. Parents need to help their children walk and grow in truth. Children need to learn how to rest and be still, knowing that God will take care of them. This is a "24-7" kind of lifestyle!

We need to get back to Biblical basics. Proverbs 6:20 says, " . . . keep your father's commands and do not forsake your mother's teachings." Why? Because verse 22 tells us that "when you walk, they will guide you; when you sleep, they will watch over you; when you awake, they will speak to you." These guidelines come with an intended result or promise. They were given to enable parents to be good representatives of our loving, protective Heavenly Father.

I think that one of satan's greatest tools of subtle destruction is busyness. If he can keep us busy, we won't have time for each other, much less God. So then, not only are we not connecting with our family members, we're not even making contact with our power source. Our families are becoming disconnected.

And when the family is destroyed, the church will weaken. WHY? Because marriage is the epitome of examples of the union between Christ and His Bride, the church. When the church and family are weakened, our nation will crumble. Look at what's happening in our world today.

We need to put the emphasis back on family time! We need to learn to say "no" to *busyness* and all those things that would distract us from the importance of family life. Teach your children to make wise choices and to manage their time well. Family time is crucial.

There are other misconceptions for which we must pray for wisdom. The three mentioned here seem to be the big ones in our world today. Let's turn now to God's Word and start at the very beginning.

Chapter Four

THE BIBLICAL VIEW

When you open your Bible and turn to the very first words of Scripture, you will read the words, "In the beginning God . . . " (Genesis 1:1). Here we have laid out for us the absolute, ultimate truth that God is the first and the last (Isaiah 44:6). We go on to read that " . . . God created . . . ." GOD is THE CREATOR! No one else has His creative authority.

In Genesis 1:26, God says, "Let us make man in our image . . . ." When God created man, He took much care in creating us special, in His image, after His likeness.

Genesis 1:27 "So God created man in *H*is own image . . . male and female *H*e created them." God knew that it was not good for man to be alone so He created a perfectly balanced partner (helpmate) for him. This couple was the only expression of God's creation that was made in His image. Imagine, you are created in the image of God!

Genesis 1:28, "God blessed them and said to them, 'Be fruitful and increase in number.'" It was God's idea for a man and a woman to bring forth new life. He wanted Adam and Eve to enjoy their sexuality and enjoy having a big family. Family was

God's idea: Man + Woman + Children = Family.

Today there's a huge "culture war" going on over this issue. **Christian, you must rise up and take a stand!** It is **MAN + WOMAN = MARRIAGE!** There are no exceptions and no alterations. We will lose our nation if we lose the family as God designed it.

The family HERE on earth is representative of God's Eternal Family in the HERE-AFTER. What we do here is important, very important. Yet "here" is just a springboard for "there." What do I mean? I mean that it's all about eternity. It's all about Kingdom principles. IT'S ABOUT GOD! It's about having a relationship with God: "He has also set eternity in the hearts of men" (Ecclesiastes 3:11). Life here is about something HUGE, something much bigger than right now. It's about God and His overall plan! And that should cause us to look up and out at our AWESOME GOD, at His Eternal Plan, His Eternal Kingdom, and His Eternal Family to which He invites us to belong.

Marriage, the union of the bride and the bridegroom, is a theme throughout the Bible. It begins in the first chapter of Genesis as we just saw and it continues through to the last chapter of Revelation. Revelation 22:17 states, "The Spirit and the Bride say, 'Come!'" It is the Bride of Christ, the church, that will be ushered into eternity.

Our **focus** and **motivation** must be on God's BIG plan! Our **focus** must be on things above: "Set your *minds* on things above, not on earthly things" (Colossians 3:2). Our **motivation** must come from things above: "Set your *hearts* on things above" (Colossians 3:1). Why? Because we have already been, by faith, raised with Christ. We need His perspective.

Going back to Genesis briefly, it is important for each parent to understand that God has created each one (male and female) special, with gifts and abilities. When the two join together in a marriage relationship, they become one. Genesis 2:24 tells us, "They will become one flesh." Each one created on purpose and for a purpose. Each one gifted and important! When joined together, they create this incredible unit called: Parent.

At the end of the book, there are some verses to help with gaining insight into what God desires for men (husbands/fathers), women (wives/mothers), and parents. It is simply intended as a "starter kit." There are great in-depth studies regarding this subject that are available at Christian bookstores.

Now, let's turn to a Biblical couple and see what we can learn from them in terms of parenting. Perhaps one of the most familiar couples in the Bible are the earthly parents of our Lord Jesus Christ.

Chapter Five

The Biblical Couple: Mary and Joseph

Although we are not given many details about this chosen couple, we can get some very solid ideas about Godly living and parenting that we can apply to our own lives and families.

First, we see that they are both sensitive to God. Of Joseph, in Matthew 1:20, it is said: " . . . an angel of the Lord appeared to him in a dream . . . ." Joseph had a connection with God that allowed him to be open to hearing God's voice. My guess is that Joseph spent time in the scriptures (study), synagogue (worship), prayer (intimate communication), and obedience (living according to God's commands).

Then we notice in verse 24 that Joseph did what the angel of the Lord had commanded. Joseph's obedience to the will of God was powerful in his own personal life and also in the life of his family. His obedience is also seen in chapter 2, verses 13-14 and 19-21.

In Luke 1:28, God sends an angel to Mary. Now this was not just any ordinary angel; it was Gabriel himself, one of the archangels. And Lord knows that if I were to receive a message like Mary did, God would have to send the "kingpin" in order for me to believe. And Mary's response is: "I am the Lord's servant, may it be to me as you have said" (verse 38). There is no question that what God was leading Mary to do was huge, and yet she still displayed that sweet, sweet surrender to His will.

Now look at Luke chapter two. There are some hints about what makes a great family. In verse 7, Mary gave birth, wrapped the baby in cloths, and placed Him in a manger. Remember, there was no room for them in the inn. It didn't matter where they were; they still made that place the best that it could be. In fact, this "lowly" place was God's appointment. You don't need the best that credit cards can buy. You just need to make what you have the best that it can be (see Matthew 25:23). And it's just possible that the world will not have room for your Godly family either, but that doesn't mean that God can't birth something great, something holy, as you bear His truth.

Continuing on in Luke chapter two, verses 8-15, there was great rejoicing on earth and in heaven! There's a celebration of life! A miracle! A gift! A work of God! We need to cherish our treasures.

In verse 16, the shepherds found Mary, Joseph, and the baby . . . a family together.

Verse 19 tells us that Mary "treasured up all these things and pondered them in her heart." How important it is to take time to think. We need to keep the vision of all God has in store for our children. They are "HIS gifts" on loan to us for a short time. Sometimes, perhaps often, we get caught up in the moment, but we need to step back, get the bigger picture in mind again, and entrust our children back to the Lord.

We see that Christ's parents were obedient to the Scriptural directives for children. Verse 21 tells us, that, "On the eighth day, when it was time to circumcise *H*im . . ." our King of kings was presented, in obedience to God's will, circumcised, and given the name Jesus. In verse 22 we read, "Joseph and Mary took *H*im to Jerusalem to present *H*im to the Lord." His parents brought Him to the temple and had Him dedicated.

The Child's father and mother marveled at what was said about Him and His purpose (verses 25-38). God spoke to the heart of Joseph and Mary and confirmed the plan for His Son through Simeon and Anna. God has a plan for your child(ren). Remember God's words in Jeremiah 1:5, "Before I formed you in the womb I knew *(chose)* you . . . ." Then chapter 29:11, "For I know the plans I have for you declares the LORD . . . ." And in Psalm 139:16, " . . . all the days ordained for me were written in *Y*our book before one of them came to be." Always remember that you and your child are a part of God's eternal plan.

In verse 35 of Luke chapter 2, Simeon spoke to Mary saying, "A sword will pierce your own soul too." A mother's heart will feel deeply the things that happen to her own children. There's a special bond, and although there is eternal victory in the life of Christ, there were going to be hard times ahead of Him. There will be difficult days for our children as well, but with God there is victory.

Joseph and Mary continued to follow all that God had commanded. Look at Luke 2:39, "When Joseph and Mary had done *everything* required . . . they could return home . . . ." There was a deep commitment to do *all* that God had set before them.

And then we read in verse 40, "And the child grew and became strong; *H*e was filled with wisdom, and the grace of God was upon *H*im." Perhaps this was, at least in part, a result of the firm foundation that His parents had laid in being faithful to God.

Joseph and Mary remained faithful to God as seen in verse 41, "Every year *H*is parents went to Jerusalem . . . ." What a tremendous example to live before our children. God must be our priority and we must remain faithful to Him. And God remains faithful to us: "The LORD *H*imself goes before you and will be with you; *H*e will never leave you nor forsake you. Do not be afraid; do not be discouraged" (Deuteronomy 31:8).

Parenting is not easy, but with God ALL things are possible! (Mark 10:27, Genesis 18:14, Jeremiah 32:27) Remember: Parenting was God's idea and He is our enabler!

GETTING PRACTICAL
Using the acrostic "P - A - R - E - N - T"

So far some practical ideas about Biblical parenting have been introduced. The following chapters address issues that are of great importance to parents and parenting. You might use the following material as a tool to evaluate how you are doing already. You may gain some ideas of what can be changed and implemented in your family life. However you choose to use this information, it is my prayer that God would encourage your heart as you see His transforming power begin to work in your family.

The acrostic PARENT will help us to focus and remember the information better.
- P = Parenting Par-Excellence and Prayer
- A = Authoritative Advocate
- R = Respected Regulator
- E = Eternal Emphasis
- N = Natal Nurturer
- T = Team Teaching

Chapter Six

P = PARENTING PAR-EXCELLENCE!

Colossians 1:18 says that Christ "is the head of the body, the church . . . so that in everything *H*e might have the supremacy." Christ must be pre-eminent in your life and in your home. As seen with Joseph and Mary, parents must be committed to Godly principles.

Our STANDARD must be the BIBLE! It holds direction, values, and principles, and it invites God's blessing. So, if you want to see God bless your family, put Him first. Jesus tells us in Matthew 6:33, "Seek first *H*is *K*ingdom and *H*is righteousness, and all these things will be given to you as well."

God is our Heavenly Father. He is the perfect "Dad," the "Parent Par-excellence." He has given us an incredible example to follow. He will also give us all we need to live according to His will. "His divine power has given us everything we need for life and *G*odliness through our knowledge of *H*im who called us by *H*is own glory and goodness" (2 Peter 1:3). God is our enabler! This is powerful, *Power-Filled Parenting*.

Jesus said, "**As** the Father has *loved* me, **so I** have *loved* you. **Now** *you* remain in my *love*" (John 15:9). WHY? Because *LOVE* is the most excellent way (1 Corinthians 13:31; see also Galatians 5:6b). 1 Corinthians chapter 13 begins, "And now I will show you the most excellent way . . . ." It makes sense then that we would want to learn what this most excellent way is.

For a clear picture of Biblical love, read 1 Corinthians chapter 13. This chapter is known as "The Great Love Chapter," and when applied, it will transform and revolutionize your relationships and your home life. One of the greatest gifts that you as parents can give to your children is the mutual love and respect between a mother and father (1 Peter 1:22, 4:8).

As you submit to the authority of God and seek to grow in your relationship with Him, He will gain the supremacy in your own life and in your home.

The other "**P**" word that must be put in place is **PRAYER!!!** Pray without ceasing (1 Thessalonians 5:17). Pray God's blessing for your children. Pray Scripture over your children. Pray God's protection over your children. Pray! Pray!! Pray!!! As husbands and wives, as moms and dads, be praying partners! "The prayer of a righteous man is powerful and effective" (James 5:16). This verse starts out by telling us that we need to confess our sins (making us righteous, in a right relationship with

God and others) and that we should be praying for others. Why? So that there will be healing.

Consider a power-pack. It is the "juice pack," so to speak, that we can carry with us wherever we go. The power-pack of prayer gets charged up by being plugged into the Word of God during our personal devotions as it strengthens our relationship with Christ. When we are in a right relationship with Christ, His power is made available to us and released through prayer. Therefore, prayer is a powerful privilege of continual communion with God.

Being plugged into the Word of God is important. Psalm 119:11 says, "I have hidden *Your Word* in my heart, that I might not sin against *You.*" For, Psalm 66:18-19 says, "If I had cherished sin in my heart, the Lord would not have listened; but God has surely listened and heard my voice in prayer." Therefore, "The prayer of a righteous man is powerful and effective" (James 5:16). So pray, pray, pray!

Chapter Seven

A = AUTHORITATIVE ADVOCATE!

First, let's look at the word *authoritative*. God has ultimate and total authority. God has delegated some of His authority, "power of control," to you as parents. You are the *"umbrella"* that God uses to *"cover"* your children here. Now, let's look at the word *advocate*. You want to be your kids' best fan, their greatest supporter. This is important. However, there is a caution: you are not their best friend, at least not in the formative years. God wants you to be an authoritative advocate.

Paul said that he had been given authority from the Lord: " . . . the authority the Lord gave me . . . ." What was it for? It is for "building you up, not for tearing you down" (2 Corinthians 13:10). We have our greatest example of parental authority in God whose loving-kindness draws us to repentance, and to Himself (Romans 2:4). It is out of a positive love relationship that our authority is used to grow up (rear) our children correctly.

How can you effectively be that Godly authoritative advocate? Here are some ideas:

Lead by example. Your children are watching you and how **you** respond to authority. They will reflect what they see in you. Paul makes a strong statement to the church at Corinth when he says, "Follow my example." Then he qualifies it: "*AS* I follow the example of *(Who?)* Christ" (1 Corinthians 11:1). Why? Because Christ is The Perfect Example! This may require some changes in your life, in your reactions, in the way you speak of and to others, etc. but it is extremely important.

Admonish. "Let the word of Christ dwell in you richly as you teach and admonish" (Colossians 3:1). To admonish means to give warning or advice in a caring way (NIV). The Word of Christ is living and we must use the Word of God to rightly handle life's situations (2 Timothy 3:16-17). Be there for your children. Develop a relationship that invites them to talk with you and get your input, counsel, and ideas. They just may want to follow Christ because they see Christ in you and they like what they see.

Discipline. "The LORD disciplines those *H*e loves, as a father the son he delights in" (Proverbs 3:12). "Discipline your son, and he will give you peace, he will bring delight to your soul" (Proverbs 29:17). Who wouldn't want that in the home? "The rod of correction imparts wisdom, but a child left to himself disgraces his mother" (Proverbs 29:15). How many times have you been in a place where a child is screaming at or fighting with his mother?

It's not pleasant for anyone, and it certainly disgraces the position and person of the parent. Exodus 20:12 says that children are to honor their father and mother.

There is an interesting concept presented in Proverbs. Look at chapter 22, verse 15, "Folly is bound up in the heart of a child, but the rod of discipline will drive it far from him." In other words, correcting a child appropriately can displace the foolish lure to evil. Now look at Proverbs 23:13-14, "Do not withhold discipline from a child; if you punish him with the rod, he will not die. Punish him with the rod and save his soul from death." Here it seems to say that the rod (appropriate discipline, perhaps a quick swat) will not kill your child. In fact, it may be the very thing that will help keep him away from trouble and self-destruction.

Scripture is also very careful to give a caution in Ephesians 6:4, "Fathers, do not exasperate your children; instead, bring them up in the training and instruction of the Lord." There is a big difference between being firm and being harsh or even abusive. "Let your gentleness be evident to all. The Lord is near" (Philippians 4:5). Use God's Word as your standard, and use God's heart of love as your source and motivation to train and correct your children. There is a right way of correction that brings about Godliness.

One area of parenting that is often neglected or overlooked is being willing to say, "I'm sorry." Parents know they are not perfect and so do their kids. We all make mistakes and need to make things right. After all, this is the first step in having a right relationship with God, admitting we're wrong and asking for forgiveness. How beautiful (humbling and sometimes difficult) it is to offer that same desire for a pure relationship with family members that we have hurt or when we have made a mistake in some way. Also, when others come to us to make things right, it is important to respond with a compassionate heart of love and healing. This is Kingdom living.

Be fair and consistent with your children or you will lose credibility. If you say, "By the time I count to three," don't count to 4, 5, or 6. There's a great saying: "If it's not quick obedience, it's disobedience."

Perhaps your home life has been negligent in establishing boundaries and guidelines. One way to initiate change is to include your children in the process. Let them give some ideas for rules and consequences. This gets them involved and you will be working together as a team. Children are often harder on themselves than parents would be. In some cases, this is a great place to show them that you are on their side by lessening the severity of their ideas and consequences.

If your children are somewhat older and are presenting a challenge, you may need some professional help to work through the process of developing a plan. Pray daily (without ceasing) for your children. Some older children, particularly high school age, have an established attitude and response mechanism. This may be harder to correct or change, but stick with them. As they become adults and maturity develops, it is very possible that change will occur then. Again, have them help develop the guidelines and rules for living in your home.

In the extreme, difficult cases, there are ministries that provide residential care which are very successful. Consider the beautiful stallion that needs to come into the corral. Specialized trainers and facilities are sometimes needed to guide them and bring them back, first to the pasture. They then are led from the pasture into the corral, drawing them into the barnyard and finally into the barn where there is shelter, safety, nourishment, and all that's needed for healthy life.

Parents are to be protectors, anchors, providers, teachers, guides . . . God has delegated His authority to you to be firm and loving.

The next section provides a "nuts and bolts" overview of family life.

Chapter Eight

R = RESPECTED REGULATOR!

Respect. A life worthy of respect is characterized by integrity and honor. Psalm 51:6, "Surely *Y*ou desire truth in the inner parts; *Y*ou teach me wisdom in the inmost place." We are to live a life distinguished by truth in everything. We live in a world that is becoming increasingly disrespectful. Where are our manners today? What ever happened to being polite? And yet, if we want to be respected, we need to be respectable. We not only need to be respected and respectable, we need to teach our children to be respectful. Children need to see their parents respect each other.

During my devotions one morning, I was reading in Leviticus 19 and came to verse 30, which clearly addresses the respect issue. "Rise in the presence of the aged, show respect for the elderly and revere your God. I am the LORD." When was the last time you saw this happen? When have you observed a young person give up his or her seat for the elderly, or a man for a woman? When was the last time you lived out Philippians 2:3? "Do nothing out of selfish ambition or vain conceit, but in humility consider others better than yourselves." (See also 1 Peter 2:17.)

During the summer of 2003, non-Christian TV networks did many segments on the lack of respect in our current culture. I found this particularly interesting as I believe that the networks have helped to create this culture of disrespect by the shows they air. So, if the ungodly world is seeing a lack in this area, how much more should believers be mindful to teach about respect and to treat others with respect as we strive to reflect the life of Christ?

We need to be purposeful in teaching our children to have respect for God, others, and for God's provisions. Listed are some areas where children can be taught to be polite, and show respect for others.
- To say please, thank you, excuse me, yes sir, no sir, etc. Say "excuse me" when you walk in front of someone.
- To not yell or talk back to parents or adults; to not cop an attitude, etc.
- To be kind to others (Ephesians 4:32).
- To be careful in speech (Ephesians 4:29).
- To not write on furniture, walls, or doors; to not throw things on the floor or ground.
- To pick up garbage when they see it. We should show concern for the world that God has created and placed us in.
- To conserve our natural resources. What we do not waste (e.g. water, electricity) will be to someone else's benefit. Recycle.
- To not take or use other people's things without permission. Perhaps children should not go

into their mom's purse, parents' bedroom, etc.
- To hold the door for others, especially guys for girls. Remember when men would stand at the table for a woman?
- To respect the Bible. It is not "just another book." It is the Holy Word of God. When I taught Bible in school, I asked the students to stand when they read from the Bible.
- To remove hats in buildings, especially God's house and during prayer; when saying the pledge or during the national anthem.
- To stand during the pledge, national anthem, or when the flag goes by during parades. To place your right hand over your heart during the pledge and anthem.
- To turn off cell phones, beepers, and pagers in places of worship, classes, and the like. How about turning the phone off at home when you have company?
- To not go into the bedrooms of the opposite sex. Unfortunately, we may need to keep a careful eye on some same sex visits.
- To respect the sanctity of life and marriage which are huge issues in our culture today. Age appropriate discussion on sexuality and abstinence must come from parents who can give the Biblical perspective on purity. Purity should be a life-style, not just in sexuality (though sexual purity is a gift that once given can never be reclaimed, not to mention the multitude of consequences) but also

in thought, word, and deed. There are great materials available to help with this very important topic at all age levels.

Also, senior citizens are not "historical," old and tossable. They are filled with history and life experiences. We need to teach our children to enjoy them, to listen, and to learn from them. I refer you again to Leviticus 19:30, " . . . show respect for the elderly . . . ."

We need to do a much better job of teaching respect *and* modeling it.

A "***Regulator***" (second half of being a Respected Regulator) is used to *set the control* or to *direct*. Why is this so important? Because the Bible warns us saying, "But mark this: There will be terrible times in the last days" seen in such things as being lovers of self and money, boastful, proud, disobedient to parents, ungrateful, etc. (2 Timothy 3). Why will these troubles come? Revelation 12:12 tell us that "*(the devil)* is filled with fury because he knows that his time is short." Jesus is coming back to usher us into eternity, imminently. Since the devil knows that his time is short, his main goal is to take you to hell with him. But if you are a child of God, this cannot happen. Therefore, he will do and use anything that he can to keep you from having a great relationship with Christ. 2 Timothy 3:1-5 lists what the devil will use. That's why it says in Genesis 4:7, "If you do not do what is right, sin is crouching at your door; it desires to have you, *but you must master it!*"

Therefore, parents must regulate the activities and behavior of their children. Titus 2:6-8 states, "Encourage the young men to be *self-controlled.* In everything set them an *example* by doing what is good. In your teaching *show* integrity, *show* seriousness and soundness of speech that cannot be condemned, so that those who oppose you may be ashamed because they have nothing bad to say about us." Teach your children how to be self-controlled by directing them and setting the controls for them, and lead by example. Remember, "fences" and boundary lines are for protection and blessing.

Say "yes" when you can and "no" when you should. You must mean what you say and stick to it. This will also help your child learn to say "no" and mean it when dangerous or compromising situations arise.

Help your children to make wise choices. In some situations, rather than just saying "no," parents can come up with several options to offer to children, all of which the parent can live with. Discussing the pro's, con's, and outcomes of choices brings understanding and helps the mind to process choices beyond the moment. When children are given choices, it helps enhance communication, it helps to build trust, and it lets them know that you are on their side. They also tend to "own" the decision and outcome more . . . it is an opportunity for growth.

There are many areas of concern where parents need to be regulators. There is an information section at the end of this book that covers the areas of health, diet, exercise, sleep, stress, media, etc.

We need to emphasize a serious warning here: the media wants your child! And you, too, for that matter! There's a lot of money to be made off of you! Our society places a huge emphasis on "things!" After all, you must "keep up with and look like the Joneses," right?

Again, God's Word tells us how to view these areas of temptation. 2 Corinthians 2:11b tells us, "For we are not unaware of *satan's* schemes." God's Word tells us what to stay away from. The enemy not only tries to get us to focus on money and things, but his war of **sexual attacks** on kids is enormous. It is everywhere, in everything, all the time. These attacks are not only directed at kids, but at adults as well. We are bombarded with assaults from TV and commercials, movies, music, computers, billboards, video games, etc.

Parents, be huge regulators! We are becoming increasingly desensitized in these areas. We have gone from a culture of moral standards to a nation that is no longer bothered by what is happening, but is actually engaging in, and even encouraging acts of immorality. How tragic this is, especially as we see it in the church of God! Our hearts must once again grieve at the evil in our world (Psalm 119:136). We must take a stand against it. God declared in Isaiah 5:20, "Woe to those who call evil good and good evil, who put darkness for light and light for darkness, who put bitter for sweet and sweet for bitter." We must not be bystanders as the world falls into moral depravity.

Thank God for Psalm 101, as it gives us some moral focus:
v2, "I will be careful to lead a blameless life . . . "
v3, "I will set before my eyes no vile thing."
v4, "I will have nothing to do with evil."
v8, "Every morning I will put to silence all the wicked in the land."

Recently, studies have been done that show a connection between TV watching and attention disorders. The recommendation is that children up to 2 years of age (even 3 in some reports) watch *no* TV. There's a warning for parents that for every hour of TV watched, the brain is affected in function and attentiveness. There is even some thought that TV watching can rewire the brain.[i] Not to mention that parents, baby sitters, teachers (school, Sunday school, etc.) cannot compete with Hollywood, video games, etc. Take heed, what we give our attention to matters greatly.

To get an idea of how we process information, let's take a look at an adaptation of a diagram author Sharon R. Berry, Ph.D., calls the *Information Processing Model* as discussed in the book *Character Quest*.

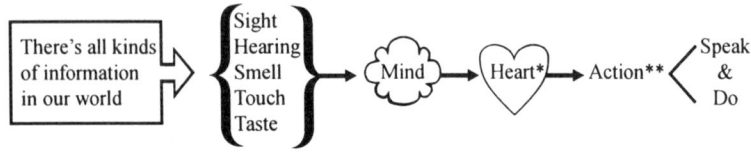

*(*my addition, **my word)*

Luke 6:45, "The good man brings good things out of the good stored up in his heart, and the evil man brings evil things out of the evil stored up in his heart. For out of the overflow of his heart his mouth speaks."

How does "good or bad" get into one's heart? First, in order to have a "good heart" we must have a personal relationship with Christ where He has taken out our heart of sin and put in a new, pure, clean heart in which God dwells. Then, our heart receives "material" from that to which we give our attention.

As you see in the model pictured above, there are all kinds of information in our world which are bombarding us constantly. We absorb that information through one or a combination of our senses, particularly significant are sight and hearing. It is then processed by our brain (mind) and depending on what we do with that information can be deposited into short term memory or long term memory. It is then funneled through our heart, and, based on what's in our heart, we act in words or deeds. Therefore, 2 Timothy 1:14 says, "Guard the good deposit that was entrusted to you-guard it with the help of the Holy Spirit who lives in us."

Proverbs 4:23 is a powerful life motto verse that addresses this whole issue. "Above all else, guard your heart, for it is the wellspring of life."
- *ABOVE ALL ELSE* - This must be your first priority!
- *GUARD YOUR HEART* - Put a hedge of protection around your most valuable treasure! How? By being careful about what you look at, listen to, get involved with, etc. Why?
- *FOR IT IS THE WELLSPRING OF LIFE* - The heart is the place where Jehovah God, your Holy Father, dwells!

Most of us spend time cleaning our house when company is coming. How much more important then to have a clean house (heart) for the King of Glory? (See 1 Corinthians 3:16 and Psalm 26:8.)

Parents, you must be a Godly, consistent regulator for your children. Guard them, put a hedge of protection around them. Help them do the right thing in all areas of life.

The following suggestions are areas geared more toward elementary children. These issues will help you to think through areas where you need to step in and help your child(ren) develop well, even as young children.

In Terms of School:
Study Area - Pick an area that is conducive to good learning. The bed is not a good option for a study place, nor is the couch, nor in front of the TV, etc. Instead, choose a specific study place. Provide a desk that is clean, organized, quiet, with good lighting. Keep in mind that natural lighting is best.

Study Habits - These need to be developed. There are great books to help with this. Help your children get organized. Teach them the importance of doing homework thoroughly.
- By all means help your children with their homework while avoiding the temptation to do it for them. They are responsible for their work. If you do it for them, not only is that cheating, but you are teaching them that mom and dad will cover for them. They need to learn to take responsibility for themselves.
- Consistent time: Discover when your child learns best. It might be after school, or after supper.

Supplies - Make sure your child has enough paper, pen(cil)s, etc. It is not fair for them to borrow from others. They usually do not pay them back, and the other child's parent ends up paying for it. This is another area where you can teach your child to be responsible.

Backpacks - Many teachers send information home that often gets lost amongst other stuff or disappears from the mind. Some parents have found science experiments growing in these canvas carriers! Make it a practice to empty, clean out, and organize your child's backpack and notebooks once a week, depending on the child's needs.

School Policies - Please also know what your school requires and help your child to respect the school and its policies. It is important for students to be on time. Not only will they miss work when they come in late, but it also interrupts the teacher and the thought processes of others. Notify teachers if your child is going home with someone else or departing from an otherwise normal routine. Read the material that comes home. Complete the "sign & return" papers expediently. Teach your child to respect the class rules and most of all to show respect to teachers.

Support your child's teachers; this helps students with respecting authority. If there is a discrepancy, disagreement, or misunderstanding, talk with both child and teacher and work towards an agreeable end that will benefit all.

Involvement at the school, such as volunteering and attending special events, goes a long way in building bridges and relationships.

Chores:
Children should have some chores at home just because they are a part of the family. Everyone in the family should help out. In addition, there can be other chores that earn an allowance. This is a great way to teach money management (tithing, saving, taxes, purchasing personal or miscellaneous items). There can be other jobs for special occasions, such as saving for a special item that your child wants. They should have to work for it. Parents should budget appropriately, and when a child wants a brand name item which is more than the generic make, the child can work to make the extra money needed for the item wanted. Gifts should be limited so that children don't get the idea that they will be given everything they want. Money doesn't grow on trees, and we should be teaching good stewardship principles whenever we can.

Apparel:
What we wear is very important. The Bible does have something to say about our clothes. In Exodus and Leviticus there are great verses about the sacred garments, the attire that is appropriate for coming into the presence of the Lord. Today, because of the Holy Spirit dwelling in us, we live in God's presence all the time and we need to dress accordingly. 1 Corinthians 6:19-20 asks, "Do you

not know that your body is a temple of the Holy Spirit, who is in you, whom you have received from God? You are not your own; you were bought at a price. Therefore honor God with your body."

Zechariah 3:3 shows a beautiful picture of how the outward appearance reflects what has happened inside. An angel said to take off Joshua's filthy clothes, "See, I have taken away your sin, and I will put rich garments on you." God cleaned up the inside, and the outerwear reflected His handiwork.

Again there's the whole imagery of the bride who adorns herself for her husband. And remember, this picture reflects the pure relationship of the greatest union, which is between Christ and His Bride, the church. We must be spotless, holy, pure, and pleasing to the Bridegroom (Ephesians 5:26-27).

1 Timothy 2:9 states, "I also want women to dress modestly, with decency and propriety . . . ." This is a huge concern today. Our culture, with all of its advertising, promotes very sensual clothing styles. Let's be honest, men are very visual and they are looking at what does not belong to them. They entertain thoughts that are not only ungodly, but that are also a type of visual adultery. In Matthew 5:28 Jesus says, "I tell you that anyone who looks at a woman lustfully has already committed adultery with her in his heart." I have often been embarrassed to talk with women (especially those

who proclaim to be Christian) when they are wearing tight fitting, indecently cut tops, shorts, or skirts. There is not much left to the imagination, and it does not reflect the holiness of God. As Galatians 5:16 states, "So I say, live by the Spirit, and you will not gratify the desires of the sinful nature."

We are not to look and live like ungodly models. We are to model Godly lives. It's about Christian character, and we need to represent Christ well. What we put on on the outside should reflect what God has put in in the inside.

A word to men here: Keep your eyes and mind pure. This is an enormous problem in our world today, and it is both devastating in marriages, as well as a major cause of marital separation and divorce. God will hold you accountable for your actions. You must take very seriously the role and responsibility that God has given you as the head of your household *AS* Christ is the head of the church (Ephesians 5:31-33; Colossians 3). Men, you know what attracts your eyes . . . . Remember, other men are looking at your wife and daughters too. Protect them! You can start by setting a modest standard of dress within your own home.

A word for the boys in your home: belts are a wonderful invention and clothes really are made to fit.

These suggestions may require some radical adjustments, or at least refocusing, but it is well worth it. As the Lord's Prayer says: "Your Kingdom come, *Your will* be done on earth *as* it is in heaven" (Matthew 6:10). We need God's power and authority to reign in our midst! His words to us in 1 Peter 1:15-16 are "But just as *H*e who called you is holy, so be holy in all you do; for it is written: 'Be holy, because I am holy.'"

Therefore, ***"Do not conform any longer to the pattern of this world, but be transformed by the renewing of your mind. Then you will be able to test and approve what God's will is-His good, pleasing and perfect will"*** (Romans 12:2).

Chapter Nine

E = ETERNAL EMPHASIS!

In 2 Corinthians 4:18, the apostle Paul exhorts us to " . . . fix our eyes **not** on what is *seen*, **but** on what is **unseen**. For what is seen is temporary, but what is unseen is **eternal**." Remember, we should be motivated by and have our focus on the things of heaven and the "hereafter." All that we do here counts for all of eternity. Therefore, we need to live our lives for the eternal glory of God.

How then can we teach our children to "think eternally?" Here are three ways to help guide our children's thinking to focus on God and to impact others for eternity.

Kindle Kingdom Kids
To kindle is to ignite, to fan into flame. Parents need to be the igniters. We live in a "Me, My, Mine" society. It's a worldly philosophy that is self-centered and self-absorbed. Recently a woman almost walked right into me as she whisked into a restroom because her first priority was to look at herself in the mirror. Fortunately, I moved so we avoided a collision. You have probably seen the T-shirt "It's All About Me" or heard those words often said in "jest." But Jesus said, "For even the Son of Man did not come to be served, but to serve,

and to give *H*is life as a ransom for many" (Mark 10:45). Nothing Christ did was about Himself. Rather, everything He did was to point people to GOD! It's that eternal focus.

We are called to serve one another in love. We are called to be givers just as Christ was. Luke 6:38 tells us that it's in ***giving*** that we receive. "Therefore as we have opportunity, let us do good to all people . . . " (Galatians 6:10). In John 15:12 Jesus tells us to "love each other as I have loved you." That's not only in the extreme case of being willing to die for someone else, but it means serving others as Christ would have on a daily basis. We need to help others and actively look for ways to meet their needs. That's a life lived out unselfishly. Perhaps you have heard the illustration: What is at the center of "sin"? "*i*" What is the center of "pride"? "*i*" But love is "*unself*ish," putting "u" before "self" -- you before me! We need to teach our children to think "KINGDOM" and about its King, the Lord Jesus Christ. Christ loved us so much that He gave up everything and He desires for us to sacrificially love others as well. That means to **really love** them with Kingdom Love.

Teach "Titchie Tithing"
When I served in Kenya at the Rift Valley Academy, the elementary school was called "Titchie Swot," which is a British term describing the young learner (student). Beginning with the youngest of children, we can teach them to enjoy

giving to the Lord! It really can be fun! "God loves a cheerful giver" (2 Corinthians 9:7). Besides, our resources are really God's, and we must be good stewards with all that He has entrusted to us (1 Chronicles 29:9-14). As you become a "giver," you invite God's blessing and will see God working in your life. Being generous also helps to lay a firm foundation for the coming age (see 1Timothy 6:17-19).

When I left Kenya, the greatest impression that I took with me was that of the Kenyan people's generosity. They live very simple lives. Some have only one light bulb hanging on a cord from the middle of the ceiling, while others have no electricity at all. Their food is limited, yet they are willing to share whatever they have with you. In fact, they will make personal sacrifices just so that they can buy some meat to put into the stew for their guests. Bear in mind that many Africans have been in our western homes and have seen what we have, which is abundantly more than what they have. Yet, it is their joy to have visitors come to their home. This is both humbling and challenging. Are we willing to share God's provisions with others, no matter how humble it may be? (See Luke 19:17.)

When we give to the Lord's work, we are helping to build His kingdom. Not only does it advance the cause of Christ, but it also helps us learn to revere the Lord (Deuteronomy 14:22-23).

Mirror Mission Mindedness

How can we reflect God's heart for the world and eternity? By looking for opportunities to fulfill the Great Commission both here and abroad (Matthew 28). John 4:35 states, "I tell you, open your eyes and look to the fields! They are ripe for harvest." We all have different gifts, and we are to use them for the glory and kingdom of God. "One sows and another reaps" (John 4:37). One gives, one goes. Why? For the eternal harvest! Why? So that the *world* will hear about Jesus! Isn't that the job for the missionary? Yes, but not only the "sent missionary;" *everyone* can and should have a mission-minded perspective. Consider the following ideas:

- Have missionaries come to a meal or invite them to stay at your house.
- As a family, go on short-term mission trips or be involved in a local mission project.
- Adopt a missionary family to pray for, write to, and even support financially.
- Support a child overseas.
- Volunteer at a local soup kitchen.
- Do some odd jobs to raise money for helping the needy in your area.
- Pick up trash in a part of your town just as a testimony to your neighbors.

We need to have God's vision and love for the world. And when all the nations have heard, then shall the end come (Matthew 24:14). The Lord will return and for the Christian, "so we shall ever be with the Lord" (1 Thessalonians 4:17). Forever!

Chapter Ten

N = NATAL NURTURER!
From birth on . . .

Children are a reward and a blessing from the Lord (Psalm 127:3, Psalm 139:13-16). They are precious gifts from God's hand to you. We believe that life begins at conception. This seems to me to be God's creative best. Not only does physical life begin, but also the spirit, which will live on for eternity. This is why it is essential to bring up children in the nurture and fear (which is the love and reverence) of the Lord. Present and represent Christ well to your children so that they will have the opportunity to give their hearts to God in faith and obedience, that they too will spend eternity with their Heavenly Father. Parents are to cherish these treasures. "For where your treasure is there your heart will be also" (Matthew 6:21). Parents are to nurture these gifts, carefully providing everything necessary for healthy growth physically, spiritually, emotionally, etc. from the birth day on.

Paul writes to the Thessalonians, "For you know that we dealt with each of you *as* a father deals with his own children." How's that? By "encouraging, comforting and urging you to live lives worthy of God, who calls you into *H*is kingdom and glory" (1 Thessalonians 2:11). Can you see how everything comes from God and is for His Kingdom and Glory? Even having and raising children, or should I say, *especially* in caring for the children that God has entrusted to us. Be encouragers, comforters, and holy examples for your children to respect and pattern their own lives after.

Each child has a Godly uniqueness about him. Romans 12:6 says, "We have different gifts, according to the grace given us." God has a plan for your children. God has equipped them with abilities, personality, and all that is needed for them to be and do what God has created them for.

Each child is different. Perhaps you have heard the expression, "Comparisons are odious." Please do not compare your children to each other. Care for them as "different plants" so to speak. There are some great "gardening manuals" that can help you to identify your child's individual characteristics and guide you in nurturing them well.

Celebrate your child's gifts and successes *appropriately*. Rewards are good when they are limited and given for 100% effort, not necessarily achievement. You want to encourage and promote growth. Encouragement is like soul fertilizer. I think we all want to hear those sweet words from our Heavenly Father, "Well done!" Some parents, however, do not express, or know how to express, encouragement, but they must learn for it is very important to express this to your children. However, some parents go to the other extreme. When parents exaggerate or over-praise the honest level of achievement, they might be setting that child up for disappointment and even a sense of rejection or failure when the real world is unbiased in its evaluation and response. Keep a healthy balance of praise and reality.

Enjoy watching your kids grow in their gift areas and encourage them to do everything for the glory of God. "And whatever you do, whether in word or deed, do it all in the name of the Lord Jesus, giving thanks to God the Father through *H*im" (Colossians 3:17). Why? Because God is the giver of these gifts and He delights in the praises of His people (James 1:17, Psalm 147:1).

As the "Provider," we should look at 2 Corinthians 12:14, "After all, children should not have to save up for their parents, but parents for their children." This is quite obvious, and most parents work hard at providing for the needs of their children and do it well. However, in our world there are two cautions that need to be addressed. The first is to the non-custodial parent. You are still responsible to provide and care for your children. Therefore, you need to do all that you can to make sure that your children's needs are being met spiritually, emotionally, mentally, physically, financially, etc.

Secondly, parents need to be careful of "over-providing." We do *not* need to "keep up with the

Joneses" or "get one-up!" Just because you didn't have such and such when you were a child, or "just because you can," doesn't mean that it's in the child's best interest. The Bible says that "*G*odliness with contentment is great gain" (1 Timothy 6:6-10). Be careful of the messages that you are sending to your children. Be careful that you are not incurring a debt for them by your life-style, that in the event that something should happen to you, they would be responsible to pay off. Be careful that your bills will not wipe out all of your assets. Budgets teach children that we should not spend more than we earn.

Let's revisit the manger scene for a moment. As the parent, you want to provide a place that your family can take pride in. However, the price, place, extras, size, etc. are not the important or essential elements of a *home*. Your responsibility is to be a good steward of what God has entrusted to you. A can of paint goes a long way, as does organization, cleaning, and keeping things neat. We want to represent Christ well. We may not have much, but remember the manger? It was the birthplace of the Eternal King.

Spend quality time with your children. This was mentioned in the beginning of the book. Family time is crucial. We need to spend time interacting with each other, building a relationship, which is often referred to as bonding. Malachi 4:6 states that, "He *can* turn the hearts of the fathers to their children, and the hearts of the children to their fathers." So, even if things aren't so terrific at the moment, it can change as you take the time to develop relationships. There's also a warning mentioned in this verse, that when this is not done, a curse will come. Spending quality time together takes time and effort. It is a deliberate, purposeful "date" - a time when you are face to face (not face to TV), a time when there is communication, expression of ideas, encouragement, prayer, enjoyment, etc.

There are many good books that offer great ideas on how to spend time together, ideas for projects to work on, places to go, etc. You can find these at your local Christian bookstore. One such resource is: *365 TV-Free Activities You Can Do With Your Child* (Steve and Ruth Bennett; Bob Adams, Inc.). Designed for young children, this book has some good ideas for projects that you can do with your children, one for every day of the year. Some activities to consider are visiting museums, rock climbing, building a sand castle, playing a game of catch, visiting a nursing home, doing projects around the house, camping, or hiking.

Spending quality time together goes a long way towards filling your child's "Love Tank," a pop phrase in the 90's. God has given the responsibility of "filling children up" to you, the parent. Their self-worth, self-image, need for belonging, and sense of security must come from their Godly home and Godly parents. If you are not filling your child's love tank, someone or something else will! There are tons of tentacles looming large around your children just waiting for the opportunity to grab them and hold them captive. Spend time developing a positive, quality, healthy relationship with your child(ren.) A hug a day goes a long way. Say "I love you" to your children. Pray with your children. Laugh and have fun with your children.

Make special moments memorable. For example, you can have a special dinner at which your child will announce the college he or she has chosen to attend. After all, this is the first major step towards independence. Or you could have a "coming of age" celebration when your child turns thirteen as missionary friends of mine do in Kenya. The family comes up with thirteen tasks that the child must complete by the date of his birthday. Then, those who are invited to celebrate this occasion with the family are also invited to help hold the child accountable as he grows into the person God wants him to be.

Journaling can be extremely beneficial. Teach your children how to write about life's highlights, feelings, discoveries, what they tried that worked and what didn't work, how God is speaking to them, how God intervened in their lives, how God answered prayer, etc. Journaling helps to process life and is a wonderful tool for remembering things that could easily be forgotten. It is an effective tool for growth and building faith.

The most powerful way to nurture and fill a child's "love tank" is by having family devotions. These special times nourish both spiritual life and family life. I remember as a child my parents using the devotional book *Little Visits With God* (Allan Hart Jahsmann and Martin P. Simon; Concordia Publishing House). I can still remember what the book looks like. We had family devotions after supper, and yes, we actually ate supper together as a family every day. There are many great tools available to help you in this most important area of development. Let's not forget that you can even have fun during devotional times, thereby teaching children that a relationship with God can be incredibly exciting.

Take time to talk at the table. Provide a positive, safe environment for everyone to share ideas, something funny, a highlight of the day, news, even issues of concern, and prayer requests. You can all brainstorm, problem-solve, and role-play to help in resolving issues that are a challenge.

Home needs to be a "sanctuary," a place where children can come for refuge, safety, love, peace, acceptance, and support. It should be a shelter in the midst of a storm. There are many storms in our children's world these days. When there's also a "storm" in the house, children are deeply affected.

They start to develop a picture of their Heavenly Father as they look at their earthly father. What picture of God are you providing for your children? When a parent blows up, they also blow up a part of their spouse's heart, a part of their children's hearts, and a part of their relationship with their family.

Proverbs has much to say about anger and the angry person. Here are just a few verses:
"A quick-tempered man does foolish things."
Proverbs 14:17a
"An angry man stirs up dissension,
and a hot-tempered one commits many sins."
Proverbs 29:22
"A fool gives full vent to his anger,
but a wise man keeps himself under control."
Proverbs 29:11

Let's be parents who provide a safe haven for our children. Along with our actions, our words are powerful. We must invite our children to live, not die. In this way we will be helping them develop a right view of their Heavenly Father.
"The tongue has the power of life and death, and those who love it will eat its fruit."
Proverbs 18:21
"The tongue that brings healing is a tree of life, but a deceitful tongue crushes the spirit."
Proverbs 15:4

> "Pleasant words are a honeycomb, sweet to the soul and healing to the bones."
>
> Proverbs 16:24

"Let us not give up meeting together" (Hebrews 10:25). Throughout Scripture, there is an invitation to gather with other believers in the house of God. We need each other (1 Corinthians 12). We need to worship together as it is vital in our relationship with God. Not only is it important to worship in the house of God, but also to worship as a family. Family worship is becoming a rare entity these days. Even in church we seem to be segregated. I understand the idea of this, the idea that learning takes place best when it is age appropriate. However, it is taking away the importance of family cohesiveness in learning how to worship God together.

There is enough that vies for family time. Please be careful that church does not become one of them. Perhaps churches would do well to provide for times of family worship. Fathers can gather their families in the home and spend time worshiping together. You can even invite other families to join. How you do it is up to you. The important point is that you do make time for this very important part of family life.

Chapter Eleven

T = TEAM TEACHING!

Proverbs 22:6 says, "Train a child in the way he should go, and when he is old he will not turn from it." Parents need to get children started on a good, solid, Biblical foundation. Parenting is a huge task and many have walked the *parenting path*. It is often helpful to get input from others. There are valuable resources available at Christian bookstores. At the end of this book is a list of contacts for information as well as resource materials.

It is important that family units work with common goals, principles, motivation, and vision. The Bible tells us that "a house divided against itself will not stand" (Matthew 12:25). Parents must work together as a united front.

God created the family to work together as a whole unit: father and mother working together for the good of the children. However, when this is not possible, there are other Godly people who can come along side and provide a supportive role in your family's life. The input and encouragement from others is important.

Parents of families who are separated would benefit by designing a common, consistent plan for household and behavioral guidelines and discipline. It is hard enough for kids to go back and forth between parents, so please work together to maintain as much stability in their lives as possible.

Ecclesiastes 4:9-12 says, "Two are better than one, because they have a good return for their work: If one falls down, his friend can help him up . . . A cord of three strands is not quickly broken." Connecting with other parents who are following God's will and who have respectful children is very beneficial. It's great for accountability, prayer, help, encouragement, and support.

Remember, you are not alone. You have Almighty God as your source for all that you need. Since family was His idea, He is committed to you and the success of your God-fearing family. You have God's Word, which holds wonderful truths and promises for you and your family. You can have the support of family and friends as well as the strength that comes from your local body of believers, the church. A strong three-stranded string is not easily broken. The stronger your support system, the less likely your "family string" will fall apart. Always remember that with God, "All things are possible!" (Matthew 19:26).

Let's not forget about grandparents. The Bible talks about telling the next generation about the things that God has done (Psalm 145) and that blessing will come down to a thousand generations of those who love Him and keep His commands (Deuteronomy 7:9). WOW! A thousand generations?! Parents, please include your parents in your children's lives. God gave a charge to them to teach their grandchildren. My grandmother was my best friend. She lived until she was 98 years old. I spoke with her every week. She was a prayer warrior for me and for all her grandchildren. Born in Norway, one of thirteen children, she gave her heart to Christ as a teenager at a Salvation Army meeting in her hometown. She came to America at nineteen years of age. Talk about a person with life experiences and the hand of God on her life and you will be talking about my grandmother. She loved God's faithfulness and loved talking about it. Grandparents are invaluable and can teach us much, and they are being faithful to God when they do. This is seen in Deuteronomy 4:9, "Teach them to your children and to their children after them." Remember, too, that your children will grow up and have children of their own. Then you will have the opportunity to be a part of that next generation as you teach them the wonderful works of God.

Chapter Twelve

THE REDEMPTIVE HEART OF GOD!

There is one more issue that must be addressed. We live in such a challenging world with temptations and worldly philosophies bombarding us all the time. So it is not uncommon for there to be many parents who wonder if their families will ever become sold out to God. Many have asked the questions: What if I've made mistakes? Have I made too many? Is it too late? Is there any hope for my family? How can my out-of-control family (or child) become controlled again? Why has my child chosen not to follow the Lord and is it my fault? Will he/she ever come back to the Lord? There are so many other situations that are too numerous to list here, but the cry of the heart still calls out to God in pain, doubt, and fear. How then should we understand the heart of God and His desire for a Godly family?

First of all, we must understand the Father heart of God. As a parent, you have a love and concern for your child that runs very deep. As the Creator and Eternal Father, God's love and concern for you and your child is even deeper. He wants to spend eternity with His children. It says of God in Isaiah 59:1, "Surely the arm of the LORD is not too short to save, nor *H*is ear too dull to hear." There is *nothing* beyond God's reach. There is *nothing* that you can do that God can't heal. Jeremiah 32:27 says, "I am the LORD, the God of all mankind. Is anything too hard for me?" And the answer is a resounding "NO!" Jeremiah 32:17 says, "Ah, Sovereign LORD, *Y*ou have made the heavens and the earth by *Y*our great power and outstretched arm. Nothing is too hard for *Y*ou." Remember the parable of the Prodigal Son? God is actively waiting with open arms for His children to come back to Him.

It is also important to remember that God's heart is redemptive. God is in the business of bringing good things out of bad situations. The heart of the redemption story is that, "God demonstrates His own love for us in this: While we were still sinners, Christ died for us!" (Romans 5:8). His love compels Him to draw us to Himself. Christ gave up His life so that we would have abundant life with our Heavenly Father. Not only do we get new life in Christ, but we are also given the Holy Spirit who lives in us empowering us to do and be all that God wants for us. Read Isaiah 61:1-3. There is healing and hope in the redemptive heart of God!

God is in the "fixing-up" business as well. I love what it says in Joel 2:15, "I will repay you for the years the locusts have eaten." This is God's promise of blessing as you understand the need to "rend your heart" (verse 13) and "return to the LORD your God, for *H*e is gracious and compassionate, slow to anger and abounding in love." As you purpose to live and parent according to God's directives, He will pour out His blessing into your home. Why? Because He must remain faithful to His word, and because He is absolutely faithful to His children.

In closing then, let's go back to Deuteronomy 5:29. "Oh, that their hearts would be inclined to fear *M*e and keep all *M*y commands always, so that it might go well with them and their children **forever**!"

And we can't forget those memorable words of Joshua: "Choose this day whom you will serve . . . But as for me and my household, we will serve the LORD" (Joshua 24:15). What a great statement of conviction and commitment to honor the LORD in all things. Honoring God counts not only for here, but in the hereafter as well.

God has graciously given us everything we need for life and Godliness and in Him alone we will find abundant life. Psalm 16:11 says, "You have made known to me the path of LIFE; you will fill me with JOY in your presence, with ETERNAL PLEASURES at your right hand."

Remember, it's all about ETERNITY!

"Your word O Lord is eternal!" (Psalm 119:89).

Do you **know** the eternal Words of the Lord?
Are you **living** the eternal Words of the Lord?
Are you **teaching** the eternal Words of the Lord to your children?

May God bless you as you take a stand to be the parents that God has created you to be!

"May our Lord Jesus Christ *H*imself and God our Father, who loved us and by *H*is grace gave us **eternal** encouragement and good hope, **encourage** your hearts and **strengthen** you in every good *deed* and *word*" (2 Thessalonians 2:16-17).

IMPORTANT INFORMATION

First, let me encourage you to read, research, and become knowledgeable in these important areas of life. The following information has come from newspaper articles, books, TV and radio programs, and pamphlets. There is a plethora of information available from both Christian and non-Christian sources. Christians ought to be leaders in these areas for we believe that it is Creator God who gave us life and we must be good stewards of His creation. Still, truth is truth, and when the secular world starts addressing these issues, it should make the believer wake up and make the changes necessary to live a life pleasing to the Lord.

HEALTH:
One in three children will become diabetic. Diabetes and other food related conditions such as obesity and all the emotional issues that go along with that are on the increase at epidemic proportions.[ii] Children must eat healthily and exercise!

DIET:
Cut back on (or, better yet, cut out) sugar and white flour.
Avoid sodas (especially diet), sweets, anything with high sugar and caffeine content, and foods with preservatives and artificial flavors. Caffeine stays active in your system for seven hours. Please reconsider your choice of the

supper beverage. Water is a must, and it also cleans out the toxins in our system.

Eat more protein.

Breakfast is a must! Even protein drinks are good. Eat eggs, salmon, whole grains, etc.[iii]

Provide healthy snacks such as fruit, yogurt, granola, veggies, nuts, turkey, fish, soy, applesauce, etc.

Invest in a juicer. Eat fruit, vegetables, and fiber.

Take vitamins and have medical check-ups.

Investigate fitness programs at grocery and health food stores.

Become educated. Many foods are grown with chemicals, preservatives, insecticides, etc.

EXERCISE:

Physical fitness is a must. Developing thumb muscles and agility playing video games does not count. Find a way to get children outside and active. Be careful of too many extra activities that may cut into family time. BALANCE!!! Find activities that the family can do together.

SLEEP:

We live in a sleep deprived nation. Our life style is in the fast lane. Children do not get enough sleep! They don't think that they need it.[iv] Consequently, they have problems with behavior, learning, brain functioning, health, safety, etc.[v] Hyperactivity can be a coping strategy for maintaining wakefulness; sometimes it has been misdiagnosed as ADHD.[vi]

For children who are hyperactive, you may want to consider the Christian martial arts. This can help tremendously with focus and self-control.

Lack of sleep can also stunt growth. The immune system can be greatly weakened.

Experts say that 4-12 year olds need about 10 hours of sleep each night.[vii]

Children should sleep in their own beds, not with parents. If they are scared, find an alternative like the couch, a sibling's room, a nightlight, parents going into the child's room for a time, etc.

Avoid caffeine from the afternoon on. It's good to wean them off it altogether.

Go to bed at the same time every night. No TV/computer, etc. for one hour before bed because they act as a stimulant. Darken the room an hour before bedtime; it helps the body and brain relax.[viii]

Wake up at the same time each day. On days off, allow only one or two hours of extra sleep.

Put bright lights on to help wake up the body.

STRESS & ADRENALIN:
Adrenalin is that "rush" or "buzz" that gives us energy. We were never designed to live in a constant state of high arousal. Our system cannot handle it.[ix] Our nation is OVER STIMULATED by video games, competitive behaviors, busyness, caffeine, etc. These "highs" lead to withdrawal lows characterized by depression, irritability, anger outbursts,

restlessness, insomnia, activity compulsion, poor concentration, memory problems, etc. We don't like these lows so we counter them with some other high level, feel-good activity. We live from high to high with no balance or necessary down time (rest). Clutter and "mess" add to stress levels. Now add to these cell phones that prevent people from ever having quiet time. Why then are we surprised by our inability to "be still and know that *He* is God" (Isaiah 46:10)?

Noise: This creates an arousal of your nerves. Your system is at "attention" which creates tension. Music is a huge concern. Too much, too loud, will damage hearing. Headsets are misused; you should not be able to hear the music outside of the ear piece. Orchestra members are starting to wear hearing devices because of the damage that constant sound is causing. Believe it or not, traffic, motors, machines, etc. all add to the noise level.

We live in a stressed out society due to world events such as terrorism, abductions, violence in the media, etc. It is important to talk to your children about these events. Be mindful that discussions must be age appropriate. Children do not need to know all the details. They do, however, need to feel safe and secure in their home and to have a simple plan for action. Resources can help you with this.

VIDEO GAMES:
Ninety-two percent of kids are playing video games. Twenty percent of these are already pathologically addicted. Games are more violent, sexual, and satanic than ever. This is sobering - ten year old boys keep images in their head for life! The killing rate has increased big time because of violence on TV, movies, videos, etc. These games are interactive with kids shooting at people, which creates an adrenalin rush.[x] A couple of suggestions of Christian games to check into are "Catechumen" and "Ominous Horizons." Digital Praise Inc. is a company that is developing wholesome games. Websites: *www.n-lightning.com*
 www.cbn.org/games

Caution: Watching TV, using the Internet, and playing video games can be addictive! Limit the time spent on these. Some children also use them as a form of escape. Help children develop their creativity with other healthy activities. While traveling, please limit time watching DVDs. Instead, try books on tape, road games, story telling, and other games. Reading is wonderful for developing the mind, skills, and imagination. But please be careful in what you allow your children to read. Get Godly advice if you are not sure or have questions. Also, reading *to* your children is important.

MOVIES:
Parents need to be cautious with movie ratings. "PG" does not stand for "Pretty Good," and ratings

are misleading, as the criteria are very loose. These ratings, however, should not be ignored. Remember, you are teaching your children life principles all the time. "PG" means that parental guidance is in order. You, the parent, must be involved. "PG-13" means that the movie is not appropriate for children under thirteen. "R" is for restricted audiences. One could think of it as "illegal" to attend if one is not over eighteen. Remember that these ratings are loose ratings, and if the world is putting cautions and guidelines on what is shown, how much more cautious should believers be since we want to, and must, guard our hearts. There are websites listed on page 74 for guidance.

I have often heard kids say things like, "I love scary, horror movies!" They call these "thrillers." What is it that should really be thrilling our souls? Horror is not from the heart of God. In fact, the Bible has about 365 references to "fear not."

INTERNET:
Put the computer in a common area where you can easily see what's going on. Use an internet filter. There are Christian internet providers that include filters as part of their service. Some filters might be OK for young children; however, some older children know how to break the block. Never give out any personal information such as name, age, phone number, address, pictures, etc. over the internet.

Filters are also great protection for adults from provocative material. Men, as well as women, are becoming addicted to pornography in catastrophic proportions. Do all that you can to avoid this very evil temptation. Galatians 6:8 tells us, "The one who sows to please his sinful nature, from that nature will reap destruction; the one who sows to please the Spirit, from the Spirit will reap eternal life." (See also 1 Corinthians 6:18.)
Website: *www.covenanteyes.com*

E-MAIL:
This is an area of great concern, especially with all the trashy, unsolicited spam. Some parents have guidelines which include a policy that they preview all e-mails. Again, this is a good reason to have the computer in a common area.

INSTANT MESSAGING:
Unlike the settings for e-mail, there is no way to check what messages are being sent. Set guidelines for your children to abide by when using I.M. also.

TV:
Put the TV in a common area and keep an eye on what your children are viewing. Cable companies can block out certain channels. And just a thought, there might not be a need for a TV in every room. I know of families who have downsized to one TV. Although few, there are some very good programs that are family friendly. However, be choosy in your selections.

SAFETY:
Teach your children to say "NO!" to strangers, to not go near them, and to even run away from them. Know where your children are and who they are with. Know your children's friends' parents. Be very cautious when considering dropping your child off at the mall or other such hot spots. Always provide children with contact information. Teach younger children to call "911" in an emergency. Buddy systems work wonders especially if children must walk to school or other places.
Website: *www.mcgruff.org*

BULLYING
Help children to respect others and to treat them kindly. If there is a concern in this area, teach your child how to be strong in character and make the right choices. There are resources available to help you and your child in this difficult area.
Websites: *www.ncpc.org*
www.stopbullyingnow.com
www.safechild.org

I trust that you have found this information section helpful. It is obviously not an exhaustive list, yet as you can see, there are many issues that need to be addressed these days.

May God bless you and give you wisdom as you develop and implement a plan of action to protect your children as you all seek to "guard your heart."

RESOURCES

WEBSITES
www.cbn.com   The 700 Club
www.gfi.org   Growing Kids God's Way
www.family.org/pplace   Parent's Place - *Dobson*
www.fathers.com   National Center for Fathering

Websites for materials:
www.christianbook.com
www.heritagebuilders.com

Websites for viewing movies, music, etc.
www.family.org   Go to: Plugged In
www.previewonline.org
www.lyrics.com
www.media-wise-family.com

BOOKS
Parenting:
Different Children Different Needs - Charles Boyd
Boundaries for Kids - Henry Cloud, John Townsend
Bringing Up Boys - James Dobson
Love Must Be Tough - James Dobson
Parenting Isn't for Cowards - James Dobson
Parents' Answer Book - James Dobson
The New Dare To Discipline - James Dobson
The Way They Learn - James Dobson
Shepherding A Child's Heart - Tedd Tripp
Doris Sanford and Graci Evans have created children's books addressing life's issues in story form.

Family Devotions:
Bedtime Blessings - John Trent
Parents' Guide to the Spiritual Growth of Children
　　Trent, Osborne, Bruner (Focus on the Family)
Teaching Kids About God - John Trent

School:
Homework without Tears - Lee Canter and
　　　　Lee Hausner
Ending the Homework Hassle - John Rosemond
Seven Habits of the Highly Effective Teen –
　　　　Sean Covey
Test SMART - Gary Abbamont

Christian bookstores are a great place to find resources. Pray and ask God to guide you, and as you look at titles and tables of contents, ask God to lead you in your choosing. "If any of you lacks wisdom, he should ask of God, who gives generously to all . . . ." James 1:5

VERSES FOR MEN AND WOMEN
PRAY: "LORD, HELP ME LIVE ACCORDING TO YOUR WORD TO BE THE BEST THAT I CAN BE!"

BIBLE VERSES FOR MEN
(Husband/Father)
1 Timothy 3
Colossians 3:19
Titus 1:6-9
Ephesians 5:25-33
Hebrews 13:4-5
1 Peter 3:7
Titus 2:1-2, 6-8
Proverbs 23:24

BIBLE VERSES FOR WOMEN
(Wife/Mother)
Proverbs 31
Colossians 3:18
1 Peter 3:1-6
Ephesians 5:22-24
Titus 2:3-5
Proverbs 31:28

BIBLE VERSES FOR PARENTS

"All the men of Judah, with their wives and children and little ones, stood there before the LORD" (2 Chronicles 20:13). This provides a sweet picture of the family together seeking the Lord.

"Discipline your son for in that there is hope; do not be a willing party to his death." Proverbs 19:18

"No discipline seems pleasant at the time, but painful. Later on, however, it produces a harvest of righteousness and peace for those who have been trained by it." Hebrews 12:11

"Fathers, do not embitter your children, or they will become discouraged." Colossians 3:21

"Fathers, do not exasperate your children; instead, bring them up in the training and instruction of the Lord." Ephesians 6:4

"Do everything in love." 1 Corinthians 16:14

"Children's children are a crown to the aged, and parents are the pride of their children."
Proverbs 17:6

"By wisdom a house is built, and through understanding it is established; through knowledge, its rooms are filled with rare and beautiful treasures."
Proverbs 24:3-4

[i] Harrell, Ashley. "Study links TV and ADHD tendencies in young kids" *Boca Raton/Delray Beach News* April 10, 2004, p2

[ii] The 700 Club, CBN. *Personal Interview.* June 16, 2003.

[iii] Davis, Debi. "Back To School Nutrition" *Boca Raton/Delray Beach News*, August 19, 2003, p24

[iv] Hart, Archibald. "Kids Need Sleep" *AACC: Christian Counseling Connection.* Issue 1. 2003 p16

[v] Rhule, Patty. "Sleep Trouble In School-Age Kids" *USA Weekend* Nov 15-17, 2002 p16

[vi] Rhule, Patty. "Sleep Trouble In School-Age Kids" *USA Weekend* Nov 15-17, 2002 p16

[vii] Hart, Archibald. "Kids Need Sleep" *AACC: Christian Counseling Connection.* Issue 1. 2003 p16

[viii] Hart, Archibald. "Kids Need Sleep" *AACC: Christian Counseling Connection.* Issue 1. 2003 p16

[ix] Hart, Archibald. "Stress And Your Child, The Adrenaline Connection" *AACC: Christian Counseling Connection.* 2002.

[x] The 700 Club, CBN. *Personal Interview.* June 16, 2003.